Elon Musk

The Life, Lessons & Rules For Success

Influential Individuals

Table of Contents

Chapter One: Early Life

I really like computer games, but then if I made really great computer games, how much effect would that have on the world? – Elon Musk

When people today talk about modern-day success stories in entrepreneurship, engineering, and technological innovation, Elon Musk's name inevitably garners much of the discussion. Musk is the name behind some of the most recognizable, trailblazing, and talked-about companies this century. He is constantly ranked among the wealthiest business magnates in the world whilst also maintaining a persona akin to a rock star which only serves to contribute to his popularity.

A look at the background and beginnings of Elon Reeve Musk reveals where he gets much of his innovative and exploring spirit. His father, Errol Musk, is an electromechanical engineer, sailor and pilot. Meanwhile, his mother Maye, is a model and a dietician. Musk's father is a native of South Africa, while his mother is originally from Regina,

—

Saskatchewan, Canada. Musk's ancestry includes British, American, and Pennsylvania Dutch roots.

Musk was born in Pretoria, Transvaal, South Africa on June 28, 1971. Pretoria, a city in the northern region of Gauteng, is one of South Africa's capital cities and is known to be a center of academic study, with three major universities, the Council for Scientific and Industrial Research (CSIR), and the South African Bureau of Standards within its territory. Pretoria is the birthplace of many other notable South Africans, including athlete Oscar Pistorius, entrepreneur Sammy Marks, South African Republic president Paul Kruger, and venture capitalist Roelof Botha.

As a child, Musk showed an early love for reading, devouring several books at a time. The young Musk was an introvert compared to his younger siblings Kimbal and Tosca. Much of his childhood was spent in the suburbs of Pretoria, particularly Waterkloof, an affluent area where many foreign diplomats resided. Musk's parents divorced in 1980, and he mostly lived with his father. Recreation included thoroughbred horses, trips on their father's yacht, and holiday travels to Europe, Hong Kong, and the United States. Although it was common for wealthy South African families to hire household staff, Errol determined early on to train his children to do their own household chores and learn to cook

5

their own meals. "I guess I was a bit of an autocratic father —
do this, do that. I was a single parent, and they simply had to
help out," Errol said in an interview to *The Mercury News*.
Musk's passion for reading eventually led to an early interest
in computers. He owned a Commodore Vic 20, a Spectra
video, and an IBM, all of which added to his interest in
learning more about computing and computer programming.
In fact, at the age of 12, he successfully taught himself
programming and designed the code for a BASIC-based video
game called Blastar. The space-themed PC game looks like a
mix between Space Invaders and Asteroid, with the player's
mission to destroy alien spacecraft carrying hydrogen bombs
and destroyer machines. A 12-year-old Elon was able to sell
the code for Blastar to the magazine *PC and Office Technology*
for $500.

Unfortunately, Musk was not spared from being bullied
throughout his childhood. Because he was bookish and
socially awkward, interested more in science fiction and
computers, classmates picked on him constantly. At one time,
Musk's classmates pushed him down a long, concrete
stairwell. In another instance, the young Musk was beaten so
severely that he had to be taken to the hospital.

Recalling his childhood experience with bullying, Musk
recalled one instance when the bullies used his best friend to

—

lure him out of hiding, and then they proceeded to beat him up. "For some reason they decided that I was it, and they were going to go after me nonstop. That's what made growing up difficult." Musk said this bullying lasted for many years with no end in sight. He would get chased by the gangs at school who wanted to beat him up, and they would follow him home. "It would just be awful there as well," he said.

Still, Musk showed resilience despite the difficulties. A former geography teacher of his, Ewyn van den Aardweg, recalls a smart and inquisitive child. "I would see him frequently in or around the library. Musk had an above-average interest in matters outside the normal curriculum, and the library — these were pre-Internet years — was the place to gain further knowledge."

Van den Aardweg also noticed that Musk's school uniform was always neat and clean compared to the other boys in school, indicating that even though he was superior to the others in intellect and out-of-the-box thinking, he put a priority on self-discipline and the value of hard work. Because his father was a wealthy and successful engineer, Musk went to private schools in the Pretoria suburbs, such as the Waterkloof House Preparatory School, an English-speaking private school with boarding facilities. Waterkloof House counts among its notable pupils the professional golfer

Richard Sterne, novelist Tony Peake, and journalist Deon Chang.

Musk went on to graduate from the Pretoria Boys High School. He was a member of the high school chess team at the prestigious learning institution, but he stopped competing when he realized that humans could not beat the computers that were playing chess. After graduating high school, Musk studied for a short time at the University of Pretoria, but his sights were soon set elsewhere.

In 1989, at the age of 17, Elon decided he would move to Canada because he wanted to attend the Queen's School of Business in Kingston, Ontario. This was at a time when the country of South Africa was undergoing much political upheaval, with the apartheid system of racial segregation being torn down. With the uncertainty in the country's political and economic climate, many South Africans were leaving the country for England, Australia, and North America in search of better opportunities. Musk also intended to move to Canada to avoid mandatory service in the military. Elon's brother Kimbal also moved to Canada shortly thereafter to attend Queen's. A friend of the brothers at the school, Dominic Thompson, recalls the intelligence and deep knowledge of Elon in many fields of study. "It's rare to have the mix of business knowledge with the understanding of

—

physics and science, along with raw intelligence, and focus. He's always known what he wanted to do," Thompson said.

It was not all smooth sailing for Musk when he first moved to Canada. He worked various odd jobs to support himself, such as tending vegetables and shoveling out grain bins at a farm owned by his cousin, cutting logs using a chain saw in Vancouver, and even cleaning a lumber mill's boiler room, a job that paid $18 an hour.

Musk recalls having to wear a hazmat suit and then trying to fit through a very little tunnel as part of the job, then having to use a shovel to take sand, goop, and other steaming hot residue out through the same hole. "Someone else on the other side has to shovel it into a wheelbarrow. If you stay in there for more than thirty minutes, you get too hot and die."

His hard work and enterprising spirit went on all throughout his college years. From his dorm room, Musk would sell computer parts and personal computers to earn extra money. "I could build something to suit their needs like a tricked-out gaming machine or a simple word processor that cost less than what they could get in a store," according to Musk. "Or if their computer didn't boot properly or had a virus, I'd fix it. I could pretty much solve any problem."

The passion and competitiveness displayed by Musk today was already very evident during his stay at Queen's, where he liked to join public speaking competitions and compare test notes with his classmates. Musk's roommate Navaid Farooq recounts their many hours of studying together or playing board games, but also Musk's superior intellect. "When Elon gets into something, he develops just this different level of interest in it than other people. That is what differentiates Elon from the rest of humanity."

After two years at Queen's, Musk decided to transfer to the University of Pennsylvania after being offered a scholarship. He pursued dual degrees -- a bachelor's degree in physics from the College of Arts and Sciences, and an economics degree from the university's Wharton School of Business. Musk's mother Maye says he became more sociable and gained more friends at Penn, particularly people who enjoyed the same interests as him, and were pretty much at his level of intellect and discourse. "There were some nerds there," Maye recounts. "He so enjoyed them. I remember going for lunch with them, and they were talking physics things … They would laugh out loud. It was cool to see him so happy."

One person who became a very close friend of Elon at this time is Adeo Rossi. Together, the two would move out of the university's freshman dorm and rent their own ten-bedroom fraternity house, where they would invite their friends for parties and social events. Ressi would convert the home into a nightclub during the weekends. He described the atmosphere as like a full-on "speakeasy" with as many as many as five hundred people showing up to party. "We would charge five dollars, and it would be pretty much all you could drink — beer and Jell-O shots and other things," according to Ressi. Despite their residence being a center of college parties, Musk was not a big drinker, only partaking of vodka and Diet Coke every once in a while. "Somebody had to stay sober during these parties. I was paying my own way through college and could make an entire month's rent in one night. Adeo was in charge ... around the house, and I would run the party." Ressi described Elon as "the most straight-laced dude" he ever met. "He never drank. He never did anything. Zero. Literally nothing," Ressi said.

It was also during his years studying at Penn that Musk developed his interest in harnessing solar power and other sources of renewable energy. For one of his classes, Musk had to put together a business plan, and he wrote a paper entitled "The Importance of Being Solar" discussing renewable energy and predicting an increase in the adoption of solar power technology as materials improved. In the paper, Musk discussed in detail how solar power can become more accessible, detailing how solar cells operate and how they can be made more efficient.

Musk also drew a "power station of the future" before concluding the paper, showing solar arrays from space sending power down to Earth using microwave beams and a receiving antenna. Musk's professor gave him a grade of 98 for the paper, noting that it was very well-written and interesting.

Other topics that Musk wrote about in college include a database for research documents, books, and optical character recognition, as well as ultracapacitors for energy storage. Regarding energy storage, Musk wrote that the end result signifies a new means of storing sizeable amounts of electrical energy, not seen since the development of the battery and fuel cell. He also postulated that because the ultracapacitor has the same basic properties of a capacitor, "it can deliver its energy over one hundred times faster than a battery of equivalent weight, and be recharged just as quickly." He was graded a 97 for this paper.

While in college, Musk toyed with the idea of getting into the video game business after graduation. After all, he loved playing video games, and he already had experience coding a computer game when he was 12. He even held a gaming internship, so it seemed like a match for his skills. But eventually, Musk decided that a video game business was not a worthy pursuit, and he could do better.

Musk said in the book *Elon Musk: Tesla, SpaceX, and the Quest for a Fantastic Future*, written about his life, "I really like computer games, but then if I made really great computer games, how much effect would that have on the world? It wouldn't have a big effect." Musk had an affinity for video games since his childhood, but for some reason he could not picture himself developing video games for the rest of his life, knowing he could use his talents for bigger, better things that could benefit more people and leave a true impact upon the world.

His ideas began to revolve more and more around the Internet, developing renewable energy, and space travel. Elon had the foresight to see that these three areas would be where he could make his biggest impact. Even while he was studying, he already had a pretty good idea where he wanted to focus his talents. "I really was thinking about this stuff in college," Elon said. "It is not some invented story after the fact. I don't want to seem like … I'm chasing a fad or just being opportunistic."

Musk did not want to be known as an investor, and wanted to stay away from the label. Instead, he declared, "I like to make technologies real that I think are important for the future and useful in some sort of way."

After he graduated with dual degrees, Musk went to

California's Stanford University, intending to pursue a PhD in energy physics. He was already accepted into the program and was about to start, but Musk decided to defer his admission to start an Internet company. It was 1995, and the Internet boom was underway. In the next chapter, we will look at Musk's beginnings as an entrepreneur.

Chapter Summary

- Elon Musk was born in Pretoria, South Africa on June 28, 1971 to Errol and Maye Musk.
- He grew up in a city that is known as an academic centre, and was educated in private schools.
- Early in life, he already displayed much of the intellect and competitiveness that have continued to define him today.
- At the age of 12, he taught himself computer programming and sold a code for a computer game for $500.
- Elon graduated from Pretoria Boys High School, then moved to Canada to attend the Queen's School of Business.
- He transferred to the University of Pennsylvania where he completed dual degrees in economics and physics.

Chapter Two: The Young Entrepreneur

I think the best way to attract venture capital is to try and come up with a demonstration of whatever product or service it is and ideally take that as far as you can. Just see if you can sell that to real customers and start generating some momentum. The further along you can get with that, the more likely you are to get funding. – Elon Musk

Just two days after being accepted into Stanford, Elon Musk decided to drop out and start his very first company, Zip2. The web software company was founded by Elon along with his brother Kimbal and Greg Kouri, in Palo Alto, California. They were able to start the company with $28,000 from Errol Musk, plus an additional $6,000 from Kouri.

Zip2 was first known as Global Link Information Network. When it was first started by the Musk brothers and Kouri in 1995, the company serviced local businesses in the Palo Alto area by connecting them with online searchers and providing directions to their place of business. The initial system used a Navteq database and a Palo Alto business database, merged to provide data. Renamed Zip2 the following year, it became an online city guide and provided licensed Web-based city guide software to newspaper publishers across the area.

In 1996, the company received an investment of $3 million from Mohr Davidow Ventures, and it moved from local business sales to national newspaper directories. Zip2 was able to score successful deals with major national newspaper stalwarts such as the Hearst Corporation, *The New York Times*, Knight Ridder and the *Chicago Tribune*. Zip2 became a big player in what the *Editor & Publisher* described as the U.S. newspaper industry's answer to the online city guide industry, competing with Yahoo! and America Online which were the big names at the time.

Two years after rebranding to Zip2 and shifting its strategy, the company was partnered with about 160 newspapers around the U.S., developing back-end online city guides. Zip2 was also providing newspapers with other services such as a calendar, online directory, and e-mail services. Another product of Zip2, the Auto Guide, allowed online newspaper users to connect with local car dealerships or private car sellers.

By April of 1998, Zip2 had become successful enough to

attempt to merge with its main rival, CitySearch. The online city guide founded in La Crescenta, California by Jeffrey Brewer, Caskey Dickson, Brad Haaugard, Tamar Halpern, and Taylor Wescoatt also served businesses in the United States. Talks of the merger soon commenced between the two companies, and the deal was estimated to be worth around $300 million.

The merged entity would have retained the CitySearch brand and brought together 700 employees, covering 175 cities in the U.S. Regarding leadership, CitySearch chief executive Charles Conn would serve as executive chairman, while Musk would serve as vice chairman and executive vice president of product and technology.

Initially, Musk was optimistic about the planned agreement, calling it a "true merger of equals." He also announced that the reason for the merger was to meet the market demand as well as to retain leadership in their category. An IPO was also planned for the merger. However, more than a month after the talks were announced, Zip2 and CitySearch called off the merger plans, with both parties pointing to "incompatibilities in cultures and technology" as the reason for the failed merger. By August of that same year, CitySearch had merged with Ticketmaster Online instead. It was later revealed that it was Musk himself who convinced the board of Zip2 not to go through with the merger.

Meanwhile, another acquisition would soon take place, but this time from a much larger entity from the outside. Compaq Computer announced in February 1999 that it was acquiring Zip2 for $307 million, with the private company becoming a unit of Compaq's AltaVista web search service. Zip2's board of directors approved the cash purchase of Zip2's outstanding shares, and this time Musk did not object. Elon earned $22 million from the Compaq sale, while his brother Kimbal, also a co-founder of Zip2, netted $15 million.

After his success with Zip2, Musk had another plan on hand. In March of 1999, a little more than a month after Compaq's purchase of Zip2, he co-founded a Web-based financial services and e-mail payment company called X.com, using about $10 million he netted from the Zip2 sale.

X.com operated pretty much as an online bank, with its deposits insured by the FDIC. The following year, X.com merged with another company, Confinity, which was operating an online money transfer service dubbed as PayPal. After the merger, the company decided to focus its attention on the burgeoning PayPal service, with a popular marketing campaign aggressively recruiting new customers who were receiving money via PayPal.

The merged company started with Musk as CEO (as well as

the biggest shareholder). However, he soon had disagreements with the rest of the company leaders regarding the direction of X.com/PayPal, particularly his interest in transferring the infrastructure of PayPal from Unix to Microsoft Windows. PayPal's core team did not like this idea, and the board decided to oust Musk as CEO and replace him with Peter Thiel.

This took place while Musk was on a flight heading to Australia, on what would have been his first vacation in several years. "That's the problem with vacations," Musk would later say, while admitting that he was not aligned philosophically with the founders of PayPal, citing Thiel's perspective in particular as "pretty odd". "He's (Thiel) a contrarian from an investing standpoint and thinks a lot about the singularity," Musk said. On the contrary, he said he is less excited about that aspect of business. "I'm pro-human," Musk said.

Musk remained on the board even after his ouster as CEO, and he owned 11% of the company's stock. As PayPal grew, it caught the attention of yet another online giant, eBay, and in 2002 eBay announced it was acquiring PayPal. Before the acquisition, the online auction giant had its own online payment service, eBay Payments by Billpoint. However, most of its customers preferred to use PayPal instead, with Merrill

Lynch and analyst Justin Baldauf referring to PayPal as "the gorilla in the online payment market".

The decision to acquire its rival, rather than try to beat it, made perfect sense for eBay. With a price tag of $1.5 billion in stock, the PayPal purchase allowed eBay to retain more control over the payment services on its platform. It was also a giant payday for Musk, and the newly-acquired wealth from the sale of PayPal enabled him to set his sights elsewhere -- out of Silicon Valley.

In the next chapter, we will take a look at SpaceX, the company Musk started out of his love for space travel, and how Musk's innovation has revolutionized rocket science.

Chapter Summary

- Zip2 was the first company started by Elon Musk. The web software company licensed Web-based city guide software programs and provided other services to businesses.
- In 1999, Compaq Computer acquired Zip2 for $307 million, turning Zip2 into a unit of AltaVista.
- Elon Musk's second business enterprise was X.com, an online financial services and payment provider.
- Musk was the CEO of the merged X.com/PayPal, but he soon became at odds with the board and was ousted from his position while on his way to Australia for a vacation.
- X.com merged with Confinity in 2000 and soon became PayPal, the leading online payment provider.
- In 2002, eBay acquired PayPal in a $1.5 billion deal.

Chapter Three: The Rise of SpaceX

The next big moment will be life becoming multi-planetary. – Elon Musk

When PayPal was bought by eBay, Elon Musk, who was PayPal's largest shareholder, received $165 million. This big sum of money allowed him to now focus his attention on something he had loved since childhood: space travel. With his pockets now awash with cash, Musk set out to start Space Exploration Technologies Corporation, or SpaceX.

SpaceX grew out of Musk's concept of landing a miniature greenhouse on Mars and growing plants. He conceptualized this plan in his Mars Oasis project in 2001, trying to shore up waning public interest in space exploration and technology while also lobbying to increase the budget allocation for the National Aeronautics and Space Administration (NASA).

In the Mars Oasis project, Musk wanted to grow food crops on Mars using refurbished intercontinental ballistic missiles from

Russia. The refurbished ICBMs would carry the payloads to space, guided from Earth. In October 2001, Musk travelled to Moscow accompanied by Adeo Ressi, his college buddy, and Jim Cantrell, an aerospace equipment and supplies fixer. The three met with several Russian companies such as NPO Lavochkin and Kosmotras.

Ressi, who was Musk's close friend since their college days, was trying his best to discourage the project. He thought of the space exploration idea as a waste of Musk's money, and tried to dissuade him by sending videos of exploding European, American, and Russian rockets. Ressi even tried to stage interventions with the help of other friends of Musk's, but his friend was determined.

Cantrell, however, said in an interview with *Bloomberg* that the meetings with the Russians did not go as planned, especially because the Russians did not take Musk seriously, viewing him as a novice. "One of their chief designers spit on me and Elon because he thought we were full of s***," according to Cantrell. Musk and his cohorts were not able to finalize any deals for refurbished rockets, and they returned to the United States. Another trip to Russia in 2002 yielded the same results, the team coming up empty-handed.

Flying home from the second Russian trip, Musk then realized that with his resources, he could instead start his own company and build the cheaper space rockets that he needed for his Mars exploration goals. Doing the calculations, Musk found that the cost of the raw materials to build his own rocket would only be 3 percent of what he would shell out if he bought them from the Russians.

With the new plan in mind, Musk set out to find staff for his space company. He networked with different space experts, bringing them together at events he hosted in California. Scientists from NASA were among those Musk consulted with. In particular, Musk talked to rocket engineer and designer Tom Mueller, who agreed to work for Musk's company. Mueller became one of the founding employees of SpaceX.

Mueller brought a lot of engineering and rocket design experience to SpaceX. Before joining Musk's team, Mueller was affiliated with aerospace firm TRW, based in Redondo Beach, California. In his spare time, Mueller built his own engines and launched them in the Mojave Desert, often with friends and aerospace aficionados from the Reaction Research Society. When Musk found out about Mueller and met with him in January of 2002, he saw a homemade rocket engine Mueller was building, and asked, "Can you build something bigger?"

It was the start of Mueller's career with Musk's SpaceX. The company now has over 6,000 employees, and Mueller is the Chief Technology Officer of Propulsion. His work on the TR-10, Merlin Rocket Engines, and Dragon spacecraft propulsion are highly regarded throughout the industry. When *Popular Mechanics* interviewed Mueller in 2009 regarding his experience working for Musk's SpaceX, he compared it to his previous company, saying, "TRW is a huge company with a tiny propulsion department. Here, I'm kind of king."

SpaceX has been at the forefront of many space rocket achievements, including the first orbit of a private venture liquid-fuelled rocket (Falcon 1 Flight 4, September 28, 2008); first company to use private funding; first funded company to be successful in launching, orbiting, and recovering a spacecraft (Falcon 9 Flight 2, December 9, 2010); first spacecraft from a privately-owned company to be sent to the ISS (Falcon 9, May 25, 2012); the very first successful re-launch and landing from space of a used orbital rocket; first controlled return trip and recovery of a payload fairing rocket (Falcon 9, March 30, 2017); and many other notable milestones.

The goal of SpaceX as a company is to develop rocket technology and make humanity a spacefaring civilization using space launch vehicles. From its founding in 2002, SpaceX focused on designing space launch and spacecraft vehicles with superior engineering. Its track record allowed SpaceX to be awarded a contract with NASA to continue developing and testing the Falcon 9 and Dragon spacecraft for transporting cargo to the International Space Station. NASA also awarded SpaceX a $1.6 billion contract in 2008 for the Commercial Resupply Services program to the Space Station, which was previously handled by the US Space Shuttle.

SpaceX is now considered the world's largest private producer of rocket engines, far outpacing the Russian companies Musk intended to work with when he first envisioned his space exploration plans. SpaceX holds the current record for a rocket engine's highest thrust-to-weight ratio (Merlin 1D). There are about 100 Merlin 1D engines in operation today in the world.

So why all the energy, investment, and effort into SpaceX? Musk believes that space travel is a necessary step in the preservation and expansion of the human race, and there may come a time when humans must occupy other planets in order to ensure the survival of the species. In an interview with *Esquire*, Musk said the next big moment of human life will be becoming a multi-planetary species, and this would serve to progress the diversity of human collective consciousness. "It would also serve as a hedge against the myriad--and growing--threats to our survival," Musk said. The entrepreneur certainly views an asteroid hit or a supervolcanic eruption as credible threats to the survival of humankind, but he is also concerned about other threats, not experienced yet, by other species, such as an engineered virus, a nuclear war, the accidental creation of a micro black hole, or the discovery of a yet-unknown technology that could bring about the end of life as we know it. "Sooner or later, we must expand life beyond our little blue mud ball," Musk reiterates, or humankind will become extinct.

Passionate as he may be about exploring the worlds beyond Earth, Musk has not lost any interest in making life better for our home planet. In the next chapter, we will explore another company that Musk founded – Tesla.

Chapter Summary

- Elon Musk founded Space Exploration Technologies Corp. or SpaceX using part of the money he received from the sale of PayPal to eBay.
- Musk's space exploration interest was conceptualized in his Mars Oasis project, which sought to land greenhouses and grow crops on Mars.
- When his first attempts to buy affordable space rockets from Russian suppliers failed, Musk decided to start his own space rocket company.
- SpaceX has scored numerous contracts with NASA and is now the leading private rocket engine company in the world.
- Musk is determined to make the human race a multi-planetary species, believing that space travel will save humans from becoming extinct in the future.

Chapter Four: Tesla Hits the Road

Either I went all in, or Tesla dies. – Elon Musk

Elon Musk already had his hands full with SpaceX, but somehow, he still found the time to venture into another company. Tesla Inc., formerly known as Tesla Motors, was started in 2003 by Martin Eberhard and Marc Tarpenning, with co-founders Ian Wright, JB Straubel, and Musk. Tesla is an automotive company known for its innovations in electric-powered cars, lithium-ion batteries for energy storage, and residential solar panels (via SolarCity, its subsidiary).

As CEO of Tesla, Musk wants to produce affordable, efficient, mass market electric cars that would reduce pollution and dependence on oil. The company is named after Nikola Tesla, the electrical engineer and physicist known for his invention of the induction motor, alternating current power transmission, and other trailblazing concepts. Musk himself looks up to Tesla, along with Thomas Edison.

The idea for Tesla came about when automaker GM recalled its EV1 electric cars in 2003. Musk said in a recent tweet that very few people are aware of how they started toying with the idea of Tesla when GM forcibly recalled all electric cars from customers in 2003 and then proceeded to destroy the vehicles. As the big car companies were ending their EV programs for a number of reasons, their only hope to keep the electric vehicle dream alive was to start their own EV company, even though it (Tesla) was almost certain to fail, Musk said in a series of tweets.

Initial funding for Tesla came from Eberhard and Tapperning. Musk led the Series A round in February of 2004, and joined the board of directors, assuming the chairmanship. Most of the money he invested in Tesla came from personal funds. Also, Musk thought of a direction for Tesla that would prove to be pivotal to its eventual success in the market.

The first vehicle designed and produced by Tesla was a high-end sports car, mostly targeted at early adopters. Musk envisioned that if early adopters bought the Tesla Roadster, and word spread about its energy efficiency and ability to beat other high-performance sports cars from Porsche or Ferrari, succeeding models which would be more affordable for the mass market would not need advertising or marketing campaigns.

Musk, in fact, is known in the industry as someone who has always disliked the traditional advertising methods. He has put most of his company's resources towards product improvement, letting the superior quality speak for themselves. Tesla, for the most part, does not spend on advertising campaigns. Instead, free cash flow into Tesla is invested heavily in research and development, engineering, design, and manufacturing, all with the goal of building the best car possible, according to Musk.

Musk used the money from the first high-end Tesla vehicles towards building even better and more affordable electric vehicles rather than maintaining a highly visible presence in mass media. He banked on word-of-mouth doing its part in spreading information about Tesla's product offerings. Musk put a premium on the Tesla vehicles, so he could rely on the superior quality of the vehicles to generate positive feedback and be the best form of advertising.

This strategy of utilizing word-of-mouth has certainly worked in Tesla's favor. Throughout the Internet, you will find dozens of community forums and online groups of Tesla's devoted followers. All are committed to promoting Tesla's brand with the firm belief that the vehicles are the wave of the future, and hold the answer to the many environmental problems facing the world due to pollution from traditional oil-powered cars.

To these passionate Tesla-lovers, they are not just buying a vehicle, but becoming an active part of the future in automobile technology.

In his statement when the Tesla Roadster was launched, Musk acknowledged that the high-performance sports car was an expensive vehicle even for its class, but the company intended to channel earnings from the Roadster to produce more affordable electric vehicles. Musk explained that their strategy at Tesla was to enter the high end of the market first, targeting those customers who are prepared to pay a premium, and then drive down the market as quickly as they could, with higher unit volume and lower prices as newer models were produced.

He then announced that the second model in the works at Tesla was a four-door family car, to be produced and shipped at around half the price tag of the Tesla Roadster, and a third model would also be produced soon at an even lower price tag. This strategy became a hit among Tesla fans, who warmed to the idea of forking out big bucks for an electric vehicle that would help in the development of more affordable electric cars down the line. Soon, pre-orders and production demand for Tesla vehicles were more than the company could handle.

The Tesla Roadster was the very first production automobile

to utilize lithium-ion battery cells, and the first EV to achieve a range higher than 200 miles per charge. From its launch in 2008 until March of 2012, more than 2,250 Roadsters were sold by Tesla in 31 countries around the world.

Tesla launched its IPO on NASDAQ on June 29, 2019; with 13 million shares of common stock made available to the public at $17 per share. Tesla's IPO raised $226 million. By June 2012, Tesla's popular Model S sedan began shipping across key markets, with Musk announcing that they were determined to show the world that "an electric car can in fact be the best car in the world." He boasted of the technology, interface, styling, performance, and safety of the Model S, calling it "fundamentally better" than anything else in its class. By December 2015, more than 100,000 Model S cars had been sold all over the world.

In 2017, Tesla achieved another milestone by briefly surpassing both Ford Motor Company and General Motors in market capitalization, making it the most valuable automaker in the American market. Tesla also appeared in the Fortune 500 list for the first time in June 2017. Considering that Musk had thought Tesla was almost certain to fail at the beginning, this was a remarkable feat indeed.

With his foray into electric cars underway, Musk continued to explore even more ways to develop renewable energy sources.

This time, he would become involved in solar power, and in the next chapter we will look at Solar City and how it is paving the way in its own niche.

Chapter Summary

- Tesla was founded in 2003 by Martin Eberhard, Marc Tapperning, Ian Wright, JB Straubel, and Elon Musk.
- Much of the initial funds for Tesla came from Musk's personal funds.
- Tesla is now a leading innovator in electric powered vehicles and lithium-ion batteries for energy storage.
- Instead of advertising on mass media, Musk wanted Tesla to focus on designing and producing top-quality electric cars, and relying on word-of-mouth to boost sales.
- By 2017, Tesla had entered the Fortune 500 list and become one of the most valuable American automotive companies.

Chapter Five: SolarCity Shines Through

To solve the sustainable-energy question, we need sustainable-energy production, which is going to come primarily in the form of solar. – Elon Musk

A subsidiary of Tesla, Inc., SolarCity Corporation was founded on July 4, 2006 by Lyndon and Peter Rive, cousins of Elon Musk. The company has its main offices in San Mateo, California, and is involved in the marketing, manufacturing, installation, and maintenance of residential and commercial solar panels across the United States. After its merger with Tesla, Inc. in 2016, SolarCity began offering energy storage services, such as a turnkey residential battery backup solution compatible with Powerwall.

The idea for SolarCity, not surprisingly, came from Musk's concept. Musk presented the Rive brothers with a concept for a solar company, and even offered to help them start the company. Lyndon was then a tech entrepreneur in Silicon

Valley, looking for ways to give back to the community. He warmed to the idea of alternative energy, and along with his brother Peter started the solar installation start-up.

It helped that they resided in California, the biggest solar market in the United States. SolarCity offered extensive warranties guaranteeing the optimum performance of its solar modules, and provided remote monitoring so its systems were always working. By 2009, SolarCity's installed solar panels were producing 440 megawatts of power.

A study by GTM Research in 2013 showed SolarCity as the top residential solar installation company in the U.S. Meanwhile, *Solar Power World* magazine hailed SolarCity as the No. 2 overall solar installation company, behind Arizona's First Solar. By 2015, SolarCity panels were generating 870 megawatts of solar power, or roughly 28 percent of all non-utility solar power installation in the U.S.

In June of 2016, Tesla floated an acquisition offer to SolarCity for up to $3 billion, with Musk declaring that it would be a seamless integration between Tesla's battery products and the solar power products of SolarCity. SolarCity accepted the offer on August 1, 2016 for $2.6 billion.

SolarCity has been at the forefront of the growth of solar power adoption across the U.S., and it is constantly finding ways to make solar power more accessible and affordable to homeowners and business owners, pursuant to Musk's vision. One of the very first solar leasing programs of SolarCity, started in 2008, allowed qualified homeowners to pay less than what they were paying for electricity from their local utility company.

The lease program of SolarCity leases rooftop solar to homeowners without having to pay any upfront or installation costs, while in return having to pay for 20 years for the solar power generated. This business model, while proving to be very popular with residential customers, drained cash reserves from SolarCity. In 2017, the company announced a shift in its business model, requiring customers to purchase the solar power systems via cash or financing. Aside from residential solar power installations, SolarCity also has commercial solar projects. In 2008, SolarCity completed a commercial solar installation for eBay's North Campus in San Jose, California, and another for San Francisco's British Motor Car Distributors, which was made up of 1,606 solar photovoltaic panels. SolarCity has also introduced different financing options specifically for businesses since 2009, and has ongoing solar projects for Intel, Walmart, and the United States military.

SolarCity purchased the SolSource Energy business of Clean Fuel Connections in 2009, and then subsequently started its electric car charging services. A partnership in 2011 with Rabobank allowed owners of Tesla electric vehicles to charge their cars for free when travelling along Route 101 between Los Angeles and San Francisco.

With Tesla's acquisition of SolarCity, where is Musk leading the partnership? Aside from the new financing options, Musk wants to make the roof solar panels more aesthetically appealing to customers, with two types of tiles -- solar and non-solar -- to be used for the installation. Buyers can customize the design based on their house's style, choosing from four main options, namely, Slate Glass Tile, Smooth Glass Tile, Tuscan Glass Tile, and Textured Glass Tile. The tiles come with an infinity warranty.

Many insiders believe that Musk's push to bring SolarCity into the Tesla fold is part of his grander plan to eventually produce a solar-powered car. Musk had already hinted in 2016 that a solar roof for vehicles is likely to be offered as an option for future Tesla customers.

For his part, however, the entrepreneur says the deal is all part of a long-term vision that one day, his will be a diversified renewable energy company with product offerings generating electricity from sustainable means, storing it for long-term capabilities, and powering residences and vehicles without the need for fossil fuels.

Speaking to the press in June 2016, Musk remarked that production of sustainable energy in the future will come primarily from solar. Combined with stationary storage and electric cars, it will be an all-around and full-scale solution to a future that is sustainable in energy, Musk said, reiterating that all three components are needed, and Tesla should be right there with the solution.

It is a strategic position indeed for Musk's Tesla and SolarCity ventures, especially with the increased awareness regarding renewable energy and the growing call among many sectors in society to lessen dependence on fossil fuels, particularly in developed nations. With Musk at the helm, SolarCity is poised to lead the way and become a profitable enterprise in the years to come.

What are some important lessons we can learn from the colourful life of Elon Musk? We will explore some of these takeaways in the next chapter.

Chapter Summary

- SolarCity was started in 2006 by Elon Musk's cousins Lyndon and Peter Rive.
- SolarCity a leading solar power installation company in the United States.
- As of 2016, a merger between Tesla Inc. and SolarCity was approved, bringing two Musk-affiliated ventures under one company.
- SolarCity's business model of leasing solar roof installations to customers will cease in 2017, with new customers now being given the option to either pay cash or purchase via financing.
- There are speculations that Musk will soon offer electric-powered vehicles under the Tesla and SolarCity umbrella.

Chapter Six: Valuable Lessons

If things are not failing, you are not innovating enough. - Elon Musk

Elon Musk has proven himself to be a visionary and an effective leader, and this is evident from the many interviews and quotes attributed to him, as well as anecdotes from the people around him who know him on a personal level. It is also quite evident that he is using his influence, the best that he can, to inspire others around him to aim for excellence and reach for something better.

What key aspects can we learn from Musk's success so far? First, it is important to have a vision in life. Vision encompasses your overall goals or ambitions in life, referring both to general aspirations as well as more specific targets. Having a vision in life will endow you with a drive to keep going regardless of obstacles that may come up. Vision also keeps you on track, lessening diversions from the tasks and responsibilities at hand, especially when there are distractions that lurk along the way and may derail you from your aspirations in life.

Very early on in his life, Musk already had a vision to make a difference in several key areas that he knew would have a notable impact on the world, including the Internet, renewable energy, space exploration, artificial intelligence, and the possibility of life outside Earth. Throughout his ventures, business decisions, and acquisitions, he always had his end goal in sight. Each step he took was one step closer towards his bigger vision.

Another key lesson from Musk is his insistence on setting the standard rather than following everyone else in the traditional path. Musk is a trailblazer who is always looking for ways to shake things up and improve the products and services that people are already using. In setting the standard, Musk is often seen as too radical or progressive, but he stands up for what he believes in and continues to prove the naysayers wrong. He sticks to his ideas despite any opposition because he already set his mind to going against the trend instead of following it.

What is the traditional, standard, accepted practice in your industry or profession, and how can you go the extra mile to further improve your product or service while also creating better value for your target market? Always remember that any attempt you make to raise the standard for your peers or competitors should have the goal of improving processes, services, or products. Intended change should be positive and contribute to enhancement and a higher level of quality.

One of the interesting components of Musk's passion to elevate the standard is his decision to share Tesla Motors' patented electric vehicle technologies with other automobile manufacturers in good faith. This came about due to his desire to really see electric vehicles take over and become the norm in the near future, thereby reducing pollution and global dependence on oil. Because of this commitment, he was willing to set aside competition, sharing the technologies with his industry peers with the hopes of advancing the entire group.

Musk, in his years of proven success as a business owner, CEO, engineer, and innovator, realized that for him to continue growing and improving in his various pursuits, he had to welcome the critiques of the people around him and take criticism in a positive way so that he could get even better at his craft. In fact, he took this lesson so seriously that he only focused his attention on the negative comments from those around him.

Musk starts off by always assuming that he is wrong about something, whether it is an idea or a proposal, and must be corrected. He is quoted as saying, "You should take the

approach that you're wrong. Your goal is to be less wrong."
With this perspective, it becomes easier for Musk to take in
harsh criticism from peers or employees because he has
already established that he needs correction instead of
walking around with a chip on his shoulder thinking he has
the best idea.

Granted, Musk almost always has the best ideas, and he is
indeed a brilliant man with a lot to offer. But he is still open to
improvement and he is always seeking out feedback instead
of avoiding it. Musk once talked about the importance of
having a feedback loop in your organization, where each
individual is thinking about what he has done and how it
could be done better.

It's remarkable how Musk still seeks out negative feedback
from people around him whom he trusts, considering how
intelligent he truly is. Remember that he taught himself
computer programming at 10 years old and by the following
year already sold the code for a video game for US$500. His
concepts for the SpaceX rockets, electric cars and powertrains,
the Hyperloop mass transport system, and other innovations
are now considered to be genius and ground-breaking. Yet at
this stage in his life, he still values the comments of others in
the know.

Be ready and willing to listen to the voices of those who have gone before you and can share their experiences with you, and be open to critique from those in your target audience who are seeking out excellence and quality in products or services they patronize. These types of feedback will be part of your learning and development, helping to mould you into a leader that is aware and willing to change for the better.

You must also look at how Musk views failure. He was not always successful the first time he tried something. In fact, he understood failure and recognized that it was a possibility in so many of his ventures and innovations. But he also knew it was part of the risk of being an innovator and wanting to change the current system, so he did not allow himself or his companies to be side-tracked by failures. Instead, he used his past failures to become more resolute, improve ideas, and eventually come out with more successful innovations. Because Musk was always looking at the bigger picture, he came to accept failure as just another outcome he must endure, so he was not afraid to gamble and put all he had into achieving what he wanted to achieve. Also, those mistakes served to give him and his team lessons on what to avoid next time and how to become better at what they do. Nowadays, SpaceX has different contracts with NASA and other private groups for its rocket technology, and is making a profit. Tesla Motors is leading the way in electric vehicle technology. The failures of the past made Musk and his companies stronger and better prepared.

Failure builds character. Character is borne from patience and perseverance, two qualities which are sorely lacking at a time when information is available at everyone's fingertips, and appliances and gadgets have permeated daily life, as people have become so used to getting what they want very quickly. Failure teaches you the reality that a lot of times, if your goal is to create something of substance, you will have to work hard for it and fine-tune the concept until it works exactly how you envisioned it to.

Consider failure as an essential part of your learning and development. The reason why Musk's ventures are even more successful these days is because they have been through very public failures in the past, all of which made them grow as a team and afforded them with more insights for improvement. Consider failure as an ally rather than an enemy, greet it with a positive mindset, and you will reap the benefits in your endeavours, much like Musk did.

Another remarkable thing about Musk and his life story, is his quest to find a greater purpose in what he is doing. Many people in today's materialistic, success-oriented society are working for things that do not really last or can only provide temporary happiness with no real or lasting results beyond one's lifetime. The focus of much of modern-day society is on earning more money, climbing up the corporate ladder, amassing bigger houses and newer cars, visiting the most exotic destinations, and fulfilling just about every luxury or extravagance the world has to offer. While these things are not wrong, they should not be all that life is about.

Musk could have easily decided to pursue a career as a video game developer, as we discussed in a previous chapter. Given his love for video games and his abilities, he could have set out to develop video games and earn big bucks in doing so. But Musk knew he had the unique position to aim for much better things, and he realized he could use his skills to truly make a difference in the world around him.

His love for reading books on philosophy and spirituality played a vital role in shaping his decision to aim higher. He once talked about having an existential crisis in his younger years, trying to come up with an answer to the question, "What does it all mean?" He concluded, after much soul-searching, that if he could take part in advancing the knowledge of humankind, and do his part in expanding the scope and scale of consciousness within the realm of human experience, he could come closer to enlightenment and reach the right answers.

This quest for purpose continues to fuel his many entrepreneurial ventures. Musk became passionate about becoming part of the solution for many problems facing the world today, including the dependence on oil, increased pollution from vehicles and its effects on the environment, and even unlocking the traffic jams of major metropolitan areas such as Southern California. Using money that he made from successful ventures in Zip2 and PayPal, he poured his wealth into Tesla, SpaceX, and SolarCity, with the long-term goal of global transformation.

There have been countless times when Musk's exploits were seen as too revolutionary, disruptive, or simply unattainable. However, he forged on and did not mind all the negative conversation around him, because he had a clear purpose in mind and he knew that one day, people will see what he was already envisioning in his mind. This purpose-filled determination is now being seen, of course, in the achievements already driving the industries where Musk's businesses are leading the pack.

A few years ago, the electric vehicle industry was doomed for failure, with major automakers giving up or refusing to even consider it as a viable alternative. Musk saw this as an opportunity to lead, and with the success of Tesla's vehicles, electric vehicles are becoming more common throughout the world. In addition, the technology used for Tesla's automobiles are now the blueprint of similar designs for other automakers embarking on their own electric vehicle programs, and it is no longer considered unrealistic to envision a future where the world relies primarily on electricity to power sustainable transport options.

Musk is also an example of hard work, and the value of a work ethic, even though he is already brilliant and naturally talented. He still puts in close to 100 hours of work every week, even saying once that an entrepreneur putting in 100 hours a week will achieve in just four months what others logging 40 hours weekly will achieve in a year's time. It has been said that Musk does not regularly take lunch breaks either, instead turning his lunch hour into office meetings or a time to catch up on e-mails. He maximizes his hours and seeks to become more productive by trying to squeeze in as much work as possible in the same 24-hour period given to him as everyone else.

Musk once likened creating a company to having a child, and said that is why he is willing to commit as many hours as needed to make sure that everything goes as smoothly as planned. He does not balk at logging many hours each week, or reaching into his personal funds to finance his ventures, just to keep his companies going during rough times, because of his intense commitment and passion to succeed.

Even after failures, Musk would show up at the office, because he knows that a strong work ethic entails showing up, even on days when he would rather be somewhere else, instead of overseeing responsibilities. Imagine how it must have been at the office for Elon Musk the day after his very publicly discussed rocket launch failures. His employees would have totally understood if he had taken the day off to just gather his thoughts or relax. But Musk's intense work ethic and powerful passion to succeed engaged him to still show up and move on, focusing on what needed to be accomplished to ensure that the next launch would succeed.

Successful entrepreneurs never stop learning, and Musk is the best example of this characteristic. Jim Cantrell, the first vice-president for business development at SpaceX and one of Musk's first aerospace consultants, saw with his own eyes how Musk devoured several textbooks at a time to learn about rocket science. Despite his busy schedule running different businesses, Musk would set aside time to read books lent to him by Cantrell, such as *Rocket Propulsion Elements, Aerothermodynamics of Gas Turbine and Rocket Propulsion,* or *International Reference Guide to Space Launch Systems*. He did not just read the books, but even quoted passages from them. "He became very conversant in the material," Cantrell said. This love for reading, of course, was developed in Musk while he was a child, as can be attested to by his brother Kimbal. As a child, Elon read close to two books every day on a wide range of subjects, such as computer programming, science fiction, religion, and biographies of successful business people and scientists. He loved books that tackled physics, technology, product design, and business management. It is no surprise, then, that Musk has reached the pinnacle of success where he is today. He invested in reading and learning, and did not stop even as he got older and became busy with different things.

If you aspire to become a great leader just like Musk, openness to learning is a critical requirement. Leaders and entrepreneurs cannot afford to sit on their laurels and just bask in past achievements. Successful people like Musk never cease exploring new ideas, discovering new perspectives, and experimenting with new processes that widen one's knowledge and expand the horizons beyond what is already known. The best learners also transform into the best leaders, as you can plainly see in the life of Elon Musk.

The best part about studying the life of Musk is the fact that he is still at the prime of his career. With all the notable milestones he has already reached, he still has so many dreams, and he has barely scratched the surface of what he really wants to achieve. Many followers lovingly refer to him as the real-world version of Tony Stark from the Marvel universe, and like the beloved character, the whole world is waiting to see what Musk will do next. His plans, outrageous though some of them may seem at the moment, could very well be the driving force of innovation within just a few years. From what it looks like, Musk is determined to take on the world and the universe beyond, and all of us will be taken along for the ride.

Now it is up to you to decide whether you will take Musk's life lessons and apply them to your own journey, or be content to just be a spectator. Are you willing to invest the same amount of commitment, passion, work ethic, self-learning, and risk as he is in his endeavors? The world is constantly in need of entrepreneurs, leaders, and innovators just like Musk who are willing to lay it all on the line and commit to positive transformation.

Too many are content to just sit on the sidelines and live mundane, ordinary lives. But true success comes to those who are ready to seize new opportunities and become agents of change. It is not just about personal gain, but about finding your place in the world and leaving a legacy that future generations will still benefit from, long after you are gone.

Chapter Summary

- Elon Musk started with a vision early in life, and he wanted to make an impact on the world.
- Musk refused to be mediocre; his desire was always to raise the bar higher.
- Musk is never afraid to admit that he is wrong, and is open to correction.
- Musk viewed failures as opportunities.
- A desire to find a greater purpose embodies everything that Musk sets out to achieve.
- Despite being intelligent, Musk works hard just like everyone else.
- He never stops learning.

Chapter Seven: 40 Little Known Facts

1.   Like many famous entrepreneurs, including Steve Jobs, Musk's salary at Tesla Motors is the very modest sum of $1.

2.   The Musk foundation is a group set up by Elon Musk that is dedicated to discovering clean energy sources and space exploration. The Musk Mars Desert Observatory telescope in Utah is run by the foundation.

3.   The Musk Foundation also runs a simulated Mars environment that allows visitors to experience what life on Mars could be like. Including waste-burning toilets!

4.   Wet Nellie, the Lotus Esprit submarine car from the James Bond film The Spy Who Loved Me, was purchased by Musk in 2013 for $866,000. Disappointed that the car can't actually turn into a submarine Musk stated: "What I'm going to do is upgrade it with a Tesla electric powertrain and try to make it transform for real."

5.   It was only at the age of 31, in 2002, that Musk became an American citizen.

6.   Musk once proposed nuking Mars. During an

appearance on The Late Show with Stephen Colbert, he was asked his potential ideas regarding colonizing Mars. He replied: "Eventually, you could transform Mars into an Earth-like planet... You could warm it up." When Colbert asked him to elaborate, Musk said, "There's the fast way and the slow way. The fast way is drop thermonuclear weapons over the poles." He later clarified that this idea was to create two suns nears Mars due to nuclear fusion.

7.   The National Highway Safety Administration awarded the Tesla Model S a 5.4 out of 5 safety rating. The highest ever given to an automobile.

8.   At 41, Musk had surgery to fix a deviated septum due to the violent childhood bullying he suffered. During his recovery, while full of painkillers, he was tweeting his future ideas about Tesla.

9.   Musk has managed to reduce the cost of reaching the International Space Station down from $1 billion per mission to $60 million. A very impressive decrease in cost of 90%!

10.   The Falcon rocket gets its name from Star Wars' Millennium Falcon.

11.   Musk was one of the inspirations for Robert Downey Jr.'s character, Tony Stark, in the Iron Man films. Downey had a tour of the SpaceX headquarters prior to filming and absorbed some of what he would call "accessible

eccentricities." Jon Favreau, the director, also explained that Musk had inspired Downey's interpretation of the character. Musk earned himself a cameo in Iron Man 2.

12.   Early on in his career he purchased an F1 McLaren as a reward for the sale of Zip2. He later went on to create the Tesla Model S, a car that can reach 0-60 mph even quicker.

13.   He has been married three times, including twice to the British actress Talulah Riley.

14.   After an expensive divorce from his first wife and during the Great Recession, Musk was living off loans from friends. He put his last $35 million into Tesla which is now valued at around $50 billion. Musk himself is now estimated to be worth $19.3 billion.

15.   He once made a guest appearance on The Big Bang Theory. The scene takes place in a soup kitchen on Thanksgiving and Musk is washing dishes.

16.   He also made a guest appearance on The Simpsons, playing himself.

17.   During a Reddit AMA in 2015, one user asked about his learning process. Musk used a tree analogy to explain: "I do kinda feel like my head is full! My context switching penalty is high and my process isolation is not what it used to be. Frankly, though, I think most people can learn a lot more than they think they can. They sell themselves short without trying.

One bit of advice: It is important to view knowledge as sort of a semantic tree -- make sure you understand the fundamental principles, i.e. the trunk and big branches, before you get into the leaves/details or there is nothing for them to hang on to."

18.   Musk has five sons (one set of twins and one set of triplets), whom he shares custody of with his first wife, Canadian fantasy author Justine Wilson.

19.   He has confessed to naming one of his sons, Xavier, after Professor Xavier of the X-Men.

20.   As a child, Musk would often gaze into the distance while his parents were talking to him. This led them to believe he may be deaf and he even had his adenoids removed. It made no difference as it turned out he was just daydreaming. His mother explained: "He goes into his brain, and then you just see he is in another world. … Now I just leave him be because I know he is designing a new rocket or something."

21.   Musk owns five mansions in the Southern Californian upmarket neighborhood of Bel Air. Totaling a value of more than $70 million, Musk ensured they are all eco-friendly covering each one in solar panels.

22.   He believes humanity's biggest threat is Artificial Intelligence. Musk worries that AI could become too intelligent to handle and eventually wipe out mankind. In an interview with Vanity Fair, Musk explained that it's

technically not a robot that would become too powerful, but a computer algorithm. "The important thing is that if we do get some sort of runaway algorithm, then the human AI collective can stop the runaway algorithm. But if there's a large, centralized AI that decides, then there's no stopping it."

23.	In hope of combatting the threat of AI, Musk launched Neuralink. This ambitious venture hopes to eventually implant computers in human brains to ward off any threat of AI. He also co-founded OpenAI in 2015. OpenAI is a nonprofit whose sole purpose is to carry out research that ensures AI doesn't destroy mankind.

24.	Esquire magazine named Musk one of the 75 most influential people of the 21st century.

25.	When it comes to humor, many are surprised to discover Musk has a raunchy approach. When naming the Tesla Model 3, Musk originally wanted to call it the Model E for what he described as "dumb obvious humor reasons." If he'd had his way, the cars would be Models S, E and X. Unfortunately, due to a Ford trademark lawsuit, Musk had to settle for the Model 3 instead.

26.	Musk stated his primary reason for starting Tesla Motors and SolarCity was to fight global warming and work towards a more sustainable future.

27.	Earlier in life, Musk would drink eight cans of Diet

Coke and several cups of coffee a day. It was how he used to cope with 100-hour work weeks during the process of setting up and running new companies. He once stated that while following this routine: "I got so freaking jacked that I seriously started to feel like I was losing my peripheral vision."

28.   Fortune named Musk "Business Person of the Year" in 2013.

29.   A user on Reddit once asked him, "What daily habit do you believe has the largest positive impact on your life?" Musk didn't respond with one of the usual suspects -- waking up early, expressing gratitude, meditating - but "showering."

30.   After moving from South Africa to Canada, a young Elon Musk was broke. He would often only spend $1 a day, living on a diet consisting of hot dogs and oranges.

31.   Despite Musk's obvious current success, it almost didn't turn out this way. The Roadster, Tesla's first electric car, faced constant production problems and SpaceX had three launch failures before the fourth and final effort was a success.

32.   SpaceX's Dragon spacecraft is the first commercial vehicle to attach to the International Space Station.

33.   Musk has the ambitious plan to cover the world with space-based internet. Through SpaceX, he plans to launch 4,425 satellites into orbit that would provide internet coverage all around the world. Currently there are only just over 4,000

satellites (active and inactive) in orbit.

34.   Along with Bill Gates, Warren Buffett, Mark Zuckerberg, Sir Richard Branson and many others, Elon Musk has signed the giving pledge. This is a promise to eventually donate the majority of his wealth to philanthropic causes.

35.   Musk is often referred to as a "thrillionaire." This is a new class of high-tech entrepreneurs looking to use their wealth to make science-fiction dreams into a modern reality.

36.   Musk was awarded the FAI Gold Space Medal by the Federation Aronautique Internationale for designing the first privately developed rocket to reach orbit. This award is the organization's most significant and has also been awarded to Neil Armstrong.

37.   Musk has developed an idea for a "fifth mode of transport." The Hyperloop – an underground high speed transit tube. Speaking in an interview, Musk claims, "It would never crash, it would be immune to weather and it would get passengers from Los Angeles to San Francisco in under 30 minutes. It would be energy efficient, maybe even self-powering with help from solar panels, which would keep costs well below an airline ticket."

38.   Musk doesn't actually have a proper desk. When speaking of his working environment, he explains, "I always move my desk to wherever -- I don't really have a desk

actually -- I move myself to wherever the biggest problem is in Tesla. I really believe that one should lead from the front lines, and that's why I'm here."

39.   Musk believes he will be the first private citizen to pioneer outer space. He also believes that the journey will cost lives. Speaking to Esquire, he stated that "there will probably be a lot of people that die in the process."

40.   It is no secret that Musk plans to eventually colonize Mars. Not too many people know what the Mars Colonial Transporters are called though. Musk recently revealed that their codenames are BFR ('Big F***ing Rocket') and BFS ('Big F***ing Spaceship')!

Chapter Eight: 60 Greatest Quotes

"When something is important enough, you do it even if the odds are not in your favor."

"Some people don't like change, but you need to embrace change if the alternative is disaster."

"Failure is an option here. If things are not failing, you are not innovating enough."

"The path to the CEO's office should not be through the CFO's office, and it should not be through the marketing department. It needs to be through engineering and design."

"Persistence is very important. You should not give up unless you are forced to give up."

"There's a tremendous bias against taking risks. Everyone is trying to optimize their ass-covering."

"It's OK to have your eggs in one basket as long as you control what happens to that basket."

"Brand is just a perception, and perception will match reality over time. Sometimes it will be ahead, other times it will be behind. But brand is simply a collective impression some have about a product."

"It is a mistake to hire huge numbers of people to get a complicated job done. Numbers will never compensate for talent in getting the right answer, will tend to slow down progress, and will make the task incredibly expensive."

"A company is a group organized to create a product or service, and it is only as good as its people and how excited they are about creating. I do want to recognize a ton of super-talented people. I just happen to be the face of the companies."

"People work better when they know what the goal is and why. It is important that people look forward to coming to work in the morning and enjoy working."

"I say something, and then it usually happens. Maybe not on schedule, but it usually happens."

"I do think there is a lot of potential if you have a compelling product and people are willing to pay a premium for that. I think that is what Apple has shown. You can buy a much cheaper cell phone or laptop, but Apple's product is so much better than the alternative, and people are willing to pay that premium."

"I don't spend my time pontificating about high-concept things; I spend my time solving engineering and manufacturing problems."

"I always invest my own money in the companies that I create. I don't believe in the whole thing of just using other people's money. I don't think that's

right. I'm not going to ask other people to invest in something if I'm not prepared to do so myself."

"My biggest mistake is probably weighing too much on someone's talent and not someone's personality. I think it matters whether someone has a good heart."

"I don't believe in process. In fact, when I interview a potential employee and he or she says that 'it's all about the process,' I see that as a bad sign. The problem is that at a lot of big companies, process becomes a substitute for thinking. You're encouraged to behave like a little gear in a complex machine. Frankly, it allows you to keep people who aren't that smart, who aren't that creative."

"Starting and growing a business is as much about the innovation, drive, and determination of the people behind it as the product they sell."

"The first step is to establish that something is possible; then probability will occur."

"There are really two things that have to occur in order for a new technology to be affordable to the mass market. One is you need economies of scale. The other is you need to iterate on the design. You need to go through a few versions."

"Talent is extremely important. It's like a sports team, the team that has the best individual player will often win, but then there's a multiplier from how those players work together and the strategy they employ."

"Work like hell. I mean you just have to put in 80 to 100 hour weeks every week. [This]improves the odds of success. If other people are putting in 40 hour workweeks and you're putting in 100 hour workweeks, then even if you're doing the same thing, you know that you will achieve in four months what it takes them a year to achieve."

"I've actually not read any books on time management."

"I'm interested in things that change the world or that affect the future and wondrous, new technology where you see it, and you're like, 'Wow, how did that even happen? How is that possible?'"

"Really pay attention to negative feedback and solicit it, particularly from friends. ... Hardly anyone does that, and it's incredibly helpful."

"If you get up in the morning and think the future is going to be better, it is a bright day. Otherwise, it's not."

"What makes innovative thinking happen?... I think it's really a mindset. You have to decide."

"People should pursue what they're passionate about. That will make them happier than pretty much anything else."

"I wouldn't say I have a lack of fear. In fact, I'd like my fear emotion to be less because it's very distracting and fries my nervous system."

"If you're trying to create a company, it's like baking a cake. You have to have all the ingredients in the right proportion."

"I think most of the important stuff on the Internet has been built. There will be continued innovation, for sure, but the great problems of the Internet have essentially been solved."

"I think we have a duty to maintain the light of consciousness to make sure it continues into the future."

"When Henry Ford made cheap, reliable cars, people said, 'Nah, what's wrong with a horse?' That was a huge bet he made, and it worked."

"When somebody has a breakthrough innovation, it is rarely one little thing. Very rarely, is it one little thing. It's

usually a whole bunch of things that collectively amount to a huge innovation."

"You shouldn't do things differently just because they're different. They need to be... better."

"I would just question things... It would infuriate my parents... That I wouldn't just believe them when they said something 'cause I'd ask them why. And then I'd consider whether that response made sense given everything else I knew."

"It's very important to like the people you work with, otherwise life [and] your job is gonna be quite miserable."

"We have a strict 'no-assholes policy' at SpaceX."

"Disruptive technology where you really have a big technology discontinuity... tends to come from new companies."

"As much as possible, avoid hiring MBAs. MBA programs don't teach people how to create companies."

"Don't delude yourself into thinking something's working when it's not, or you're gonna get fixated on a bad solution."

"If something has to be designed and invented, and you have to figure out how to ensure that the value of the thing you create is greater than the cost of the inputs, then that is probably my core skill."

"I always have optimism, but I'm realistic. It was not with the expectation of great success that I started Tesla or SpaceX... It's just that I thought they were important enough to do anyway.

"Going from PayPal, I thought: 'Well, what are some of the other problems that are likely to most affect the future of humanity?' Not from the perspective, 'What's the best way to make money?"

"(Physics is) a good framework for thinking. ... Boil things down to their fundamental truths and reason up from there."

"You want to have a future where you're expecting things to be better, not one where you're expecting things to be worse."

"You have to be pretty driven to make it happen. Otherwise, you will just make yourself miserable."

"If you go back a few hundred years, what we take for granted today would seem like magic – being able to talk to people over long distances, to transmit images, flying, accessing vast amounts of data like an oracle. These are all things that would have been considered magic a few hundred years ago."

"Let's think beyond the normal stuff and have an environment where that sort of thinking is encouraged and

rewarded and where it's okay to fail as well. Because when you try new things, you try this idea, that idea... well a large number of them are not gonna work, and that has to be okay. If every time somebody comes up with an idea it has to be successful, you're not gonna get people coming up with ideas."

"I came to the conclusion that we should aspire to increase the scope and scale of human consciousness in order to better understand what questions to ask. Really, the only thing that makes sense is to strive for greater collective enlightenment."

"Patience is a virtue, and I'm learning patience. It's a tough lesson."

"When I was in college, I wanted to be involved in things that would change the world. Now I am."

"I think it's very important to have a feedback loop, where you're constantly thinking about what you've done and how you could be doing it better. I think that's the single best piece of advice:

constantly think about how you could be doing things better and questioning yourself."

"Life is too short for long-term grudges."

"I think life on Earth must be about more than just solving problems... It's got to be something inspiring, even if it is vicarious."

"The idea of lying on a beach as my main thing just sounds like the worst. It sounds horrible to me. I would go bonkers. I would have to be on serious drugs. I'd be super-duper bored. I like high intensity."

"Don't be afraid of new arenas."

"I think it is possible for ordinary people to choose to be extraordinary."

"I could either watch it happen or be a part of it."

"Being an Entrepreneur is like eating glass and staring into the abyss of death"

Chapter Nine: Elon Musk's 15 Rules for Success

Work Ridiculously Hard.

Musk is known for his fierce work ethic. Even present day as a global superstar he is still putting in 100-hour work weeks, splitting his time between Tesla and SpaceX. Back when Elon and his brother co-founded PayPal, they would sleep in the office and shower at the local YMCA. He believes this is the bedrock to his success and there is no getting around it.

 "Work like hell. I mean you just have to put in 80 to 100 hour weeks every week. [This] improves the odds of success. If other people are putting in 40 hour work weeks and you're putting in 100 hour work weeks, then even if you're doing the same thing you know that… you will achieve in 4 months what it takes them a year to achieve."

Be a Trendsetter.

Instead of competing with others in well established markets, Musk prefers to solve problems in emerging markets that have little competition. During it's early years, PayPal was the only email money transferring system in the world. Tesla was created just as electric cars were being written off and SpaceX is the first private company to send a spacecraft to the International Space Station.

Focus on innovation instead of competition. If you innovate correctly, there will be no competition. Creating a monopoly leads to lasting value and reaps the majority of the rewards available in that particular market segment.

Make Failure an Option.

"Failure is an option here. If things are not failing, you are not innovating enough."

Originally, Musk believed Tesla would fail. Why would he start a company he believed almost certain to fail? Musk's answer:

"If something is important enough you should try even if the probable outcome is failure."

Electric cars were seen as slow and ugly. Musk took on the difficult task of changing almost the entire populations opinion on them. It was no easy feat but the introduction The Tesla Model S achieved this topping Consumer Reports' annual customer satisfaction ratings two years in a row.

Focus on Work that is Important to You.

At the age of 27 Elon sold Zip2 to Compaq for $307 million dollars. He personally netted $22 million dollars from the sale, quite easily enough to retire on. Instead he decided to continue on, working harder than ever because he recognizes the importance of his work and how he his changing the world in the process. Working on projects that are important to you can provide the best of both worlds - financial rewards and job satisfaction.

Focus on Signal over Noise.

Musk firmly believes the quality of the product or service should always come first. An amazing product is the best type of marketing there is. In his commencement speech at USC in 2014, Musk states:

"A lot of companies spend money on things that don't actually make the product better. For example, at Tesla we've never spent any money on advertising. We put all the money into R+D, and manufacturing and design to try to make the car as good as possible. And I think that's the way to go. For any given company just keep thinking 'are the efforts that people are expending resulting in a better product or service?' If they're not – stop those efforts."

Create a superior product above all else.

Seek out Constructive Criticism.

Nobody enjoys to have their work criticized as it can often feel like a personal attack upon yourself. Musk is able to take his ego out of the equation and realize that constructive criticism is essential to improvement. Through seeking out this information you gain valuable information from a whole set of fresh eyes as to which areas need to be improved. Musk expands upon this point in an interview he gave.

"I think it's important for people to pay close attention to negative feedback and rather than ignore negative feedback, you have to listen to it carefully. Ignore it if the underlying reason for the negative feedback doesn't make sense but otherwise, people should adjust their behavior. I'm not perfect at it, for sure, but I do think it's really important to solicit negative feedback, particularly from people who have your best interest in mind."

Attract Great People

A company is just a group of people working together to create a service or product. During his commencement speech at USC, Musk stated that the most important part of creating a company is to attract the right people. He further explains, "depending upon how talented and hardworking that group is, and the degree to which they're focused cohesively in a good direction, that will determine the success of the company. So do everything you can to gather great people if you're creating a company." If you have no desire in creating a company Musk instead advises, "Join a group that is amazing that you really respect."

Invest Profits into new Businesses.

Whenever Musk cashes in on one of his companies for millions, he has always invested at least 45% of his earnings into a brand new business within a 12-month period. After banking $22 million for the sale of Zip2, Musk invested $10 million into creating X.com (eventually PayPal). The sale of PayPal netted Musk a cool $165 million, he would go on to invest $100 million of that into the founding of SpaceX. Musk never believes he has 'made it', each success is just a stepping stone onto bigger and more important challenges.

Be Tenacious.

Tenacious Definition: Adjective. Not readily relinquishing a position, principle, or course of action; determined.

Tesla and SpaceX have both been on the verge of bankruptcy. The determination shown by Musk is a big part of the reason they are both now thriving.

The SpaceX Falcon 1 launch was initially a success, the vehicle made it through the most complex stage of breaking away from Earth's gravitational pull. Soon after, the rocket failed and communication was lost. The mission was a failure.

The 300+ individuals in attendance who had worked on the project thought it was game over. Musk promptly stood up and started to speak to the crowd, reassuring them he had secured more funding for future launches. He concluded the speech by proclaiming not what his employees should do, but what he was going to do. "For my part, I will never give up... and I mean never."

As we all know, the next launch was a success.

Reason from First Principles over Analogy.

Large battery packs are expensive to make; therefore, they will always cost a lot. This is logical and would be the thinking of most. Not Musk. Musk believes in stripping things back to first principles. When you strip back the components of batteries, (nickel, aluminum, cobalt, carbon etc.) these are not actually expensive parts and if made by yourself, costs can be dramatically reduced. Common thought goes: "That's just how it is, always has been and always will be." Musk advises us to challenge reality and to dive deep into the fundamentals. "I think it's important to reason from first principles rather than by analogy. The normal way we conduct our lives is we reason by analogy. [With analogy] we are doing this because it's like something else that was done, or it is like what other people are doing. [With first principles] you boil things down to the most fundamental truths…and then reason up from there."

Be Overly Ambitious.

It doesn't come much more ambitious than planning to colonize mars. When Musk initially publicized his plans, most thought he was crazy. After the success of SpaceX and securing a $1.6 billion contract with NASA, his plan is starting to look a lot more realistic. This isn't just a business decision for Musk but a potential savior for the human race. He has revealed he hopes to have established a colony on Mars by 2040, with a population of 80,000.

Improvise.

There will always be roadblocks on the road to success, this is where improvisation is key. When the Russians wouldn't sell Elon the intercontinental ballistic missiles he needed, he built his own. When SpaceX was told they would need to wait before launching rockets in the U.S, he went and found a Pacific island he could use immediately. When Tesla needed to test a prototype model in cold conditions, he hired an ice-cream truck with a big refrigerated trailer. The problems will always be there, but if you are willing to improvise, they can nearly always be overcome.

Begin with a Premium Product.

The strategy Musk used with the creation Tesla was quite unique, but worked perfectly. Step one started by creating a premium product to the very rich with the high end luxury Tesla. This changed the general view of electric cars being uncool and slow and the revenues from this model provided the funds for step two. This was the creation of the mid-priced, mid-volume produced models which then produced the funds for the low priced, high volume cars available for the masses.

Constantly Improve.

Musk believes in the Japanese concept of Kaizen, translated to constant improvement. When asked about the single best piece of advice he could give to someone, Musk advised: "Constantly think about how you can be doing things better." The only thing better than a perfectly executed plan is perfect execution of a better plan. Start by finding your drive and refining your execution, then think about how you can do things better and question how your plan can be improved.

Take Risks.

All worthwhile achievements come with an element of risk. Through following the previous 14 principles, risks can be lowered but never wiped out completely. Greater risks, usually have the potential to provide greater rewards but you should always weigh up the pros and cons. When Musk poured so much of his money into SpaceX and Tesla, at one point he had to borrow money off friends just to cover his living expenses. Today SpaceX, Tesla, and Solar City are thriving and Elon is several billion dollars wealthier.

Conclusion

The amazing thing about Elon Musk isn't his achievements, it's his persistence through the failures in his life. He had so many setbacks, catastrophes, and so much hardship in his life that it's amazing to see how he overcame all of life's challenges.

That's what makes Elon Musk. It's his *tenacity*, *determination*, and *inability* to consider **failure** that has allowed him to **succeed**.

Thanks for checking out my book. I hope you found this of value and enjoyed it. If this was the case, head to my author page for more like this. Before you go, I have one small favor to ask…

Would you take 60 seconds and write a quick blurb about this book on Amazon?

Reviews are the best way for independent authors (like me) to get noticed, sell more books, and it gives me the motivation to continue producing. I also read every review and use the feedback to write future revisions – and even future books. Thanks again.

Printed in Great Britain
by Amazon